GW01219544

VICTOR G. AMBRUS
Under the Double Eagle

THREE CENTURIES OF HISTORY
IN AUSTRIA AND HUNGARY

TEXT BY VICTOR G. AMBRUS
AND DONALD LINDSAY

*Officer of the Hungarian Noble Guard
in full-dress uniform 1782*

Oxford New York Toronto Melbourne
OXFORD UNIVERSITY PRESS · 1980

Prologue: The House of Habsburg

In the year 1020 the castle of Habsburg, or Hawk's Castle, was built in a small village near Aargau in north-west Switzerland. It was here that the story of this German family starts. No other family has left so deep a mark on European history. So powerful did the Habsburgs quickly become that in 1273 Count Rudolf Habsburg was elected King of the Germans and Holy Roman Emperor. This latter title no longer meant much but it still gave its holder some prestige if he himself was a strong ruler. In 1278 Rudolf conquered Austria and the age long connection of the Habsburgs with Austria began.

'Wars may be waged by others,' it used to be said, 'you, happy Austria, marry.' By cleverly arranging marriages with other powerful families Habsburg territory increased steadily. From about 1450 they adopted as their motto the five vowels A.E.I.O.U., which were the first letters of five Latin words. 'Austriae est imperare orbi universo', or 'Austria is destined to rule the world'. In 1519 this boast seemed to have come true when the Emperor Charles V ruled over central Europe, much of Italy, and also Spain with its New World possessions.

However, on Charles's death the Habsburg lands were divided between two branches of the family. It is with the German not the Spanish Habsburgs that we are concerned and we begin the story a century later in 1658 when Leopold I succeeded to the throne of Austria. Like other Habsburg emperors Leopold found his country threatened by Turkish advances. Christian Europe looked to the Habsburgs for defence against the infidel.

It is a pleasure to congratulate Mr. Ambrus on a work which shows events in the history of Austria-Hungary so well. He has revived a great past, which will please all who have a sense of history.

Otto von Habsburg, son of the last Austrian Emperor

Leopold saves Europe from the Turks

Small in stature, with the typical Habsburg protruding lower lip and jaw, Leopold I at the age of eighteen was unimpressive in appearance. Surrounded by many enemies, he was always afraid of losing his throne. The Turks were once again advancing on Vienna, his capital. The Hungarians were rebellious. King Louis XIV intended that France with its Bourbon monarchy should dominate Europe, not Austria and the Habsburgs. Louis bribed the Hungarians to keep Leopold occupied to the East, while with the finest army in Europe he threatened the Empire all along the Rhine. Although timid and no soldier, Leopold was not stupid. He made clever use of other people and ensured that the Austrian Empire emerged from danger stronger than before.

For over a century Christian Europe had been threatened by the Turks. They occupied all of the Balkans and much of Hungary. Turkey had a huge professional army of which the flower was the corps of Janissaries, distinguished by a high head-dress with a trailing cloth decoration behind. They were recruited from young Christian boys, seized on raids in the Balkans. Janissaries were brought up in special schools, forced to become Mohammedans and forbidden to marry. They were trained to become the most devoted and cruel shock-troops of the Turkish Sultan, burning occupied towns and massacring the inhabitants or driving women and children to slavery.

In 1529 a Turkish army had besieged Vienna without success. In 1683 the Grand Vizier of Turkey, Kara Mustafa, planned not only to overrun Austria but to advance across Europe, and at the head of 300,000 men surrounded Vienna. Leopold and part of the population fled, leaving the defence of the city walls to a small garrison and the remaining citizens. For two months the siege went on. Food became dangerously scarce. Leopold was desperately trying to organise an army to relieve the city before it was too late. It was a race against time. Eventually King John Sobieski of Poland answered the appeals of Leopold and the Pope to join forces with Duke Charles of Lorraine, who commanded Leopold's army.

Charge of the Polish Hussars

It was not a moment too soon.

The Turks had undermined the walls, resistance was nearly at an end. Imperialist and Polish troops fell on the Turks inflicting terrible slaughter. The Polish hussars, with wing-like decoration on their armour, seemed like flying demons to the panicking Turkish army. Vienna was saved.

Leopold on the battlefield

On the day after Vienna had been relieved Leopold, dressed as usual in black, rode across the battlefield to meet the victorious Sobieski. He read out a message of thanks in Latin and Sobieski politely replied. Leopold then rode back to Vienna, his mind full of plans for rebuilding the shattered city, hailed, a little undeservedly, as the saviour of Europe.

In the following years Vienna was transformed. Magnificent new buildings of every kind were planned. Most of this great design had to be completed by his sons but Leopold laid the foundations. The mediaeval clutter of streets was cleared away and he even introduced street lighting.

The army also was reorganised. The driving force behind this was Prince Eugène of Savoy. Eugène had once offered his services to Louis XIV but had been turned down.

Foolishly, Louis saw nothing in this frail little soldier, soon to be one of the great military leaders of the day. So Eugène volunteered to fight for Leopold.

Having taken part in the relief of Vienna, Eugène took command of the Austrian and Hungarian forces. Sobieski had struck the first vital blow against the Turks and now Eugène moved along the Danube winning victory after victory. Buda fell in 1686 and his crowning triumph came at Zenta in 1699. Now free from Turkish rule, Hungary was annexed by Leopold to become part of the Austrian Empire.

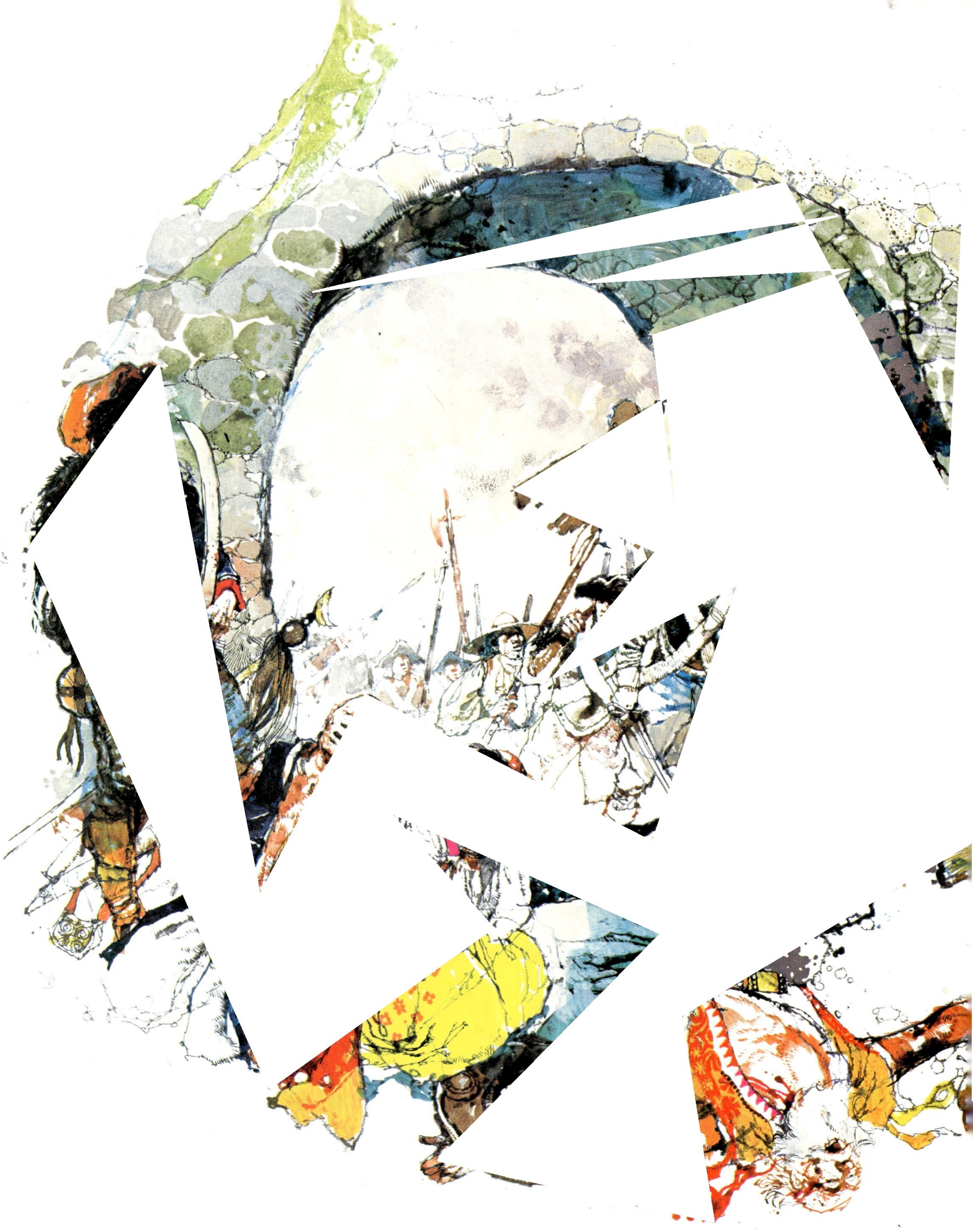

Prince Eugène and the fall of Buda

Besieged for three months by 80,000 troops, Buda fell in September 1686 when the Hungarians broke through the Vienna Gate. Imperial troops poured into the city and found that the Turks had built a huge barracks and baths. Turkish merchants and richly dressed women with their servants were captured but their lives were spared. Two hundred houses were in ruins and over all hung the stench of death. Mercenary soldiers, camp followers and other rabble looted the town, but after three days Buda had to be set alight to stop the spread of infection from bodies lying in the streets.

The Emperor Charles with the Imperial State Crown and Regalia

Joseph I, Rakoczi and Charles VI

Hungary was free from the Turks but Habsburg rule was harsh and unsympathetic to Hungarian hopes of independence. To make quite clear that the Habsburgs intended to hold on to Hungary Leopold I dressed his nine year old son, Joseph, in richly embroidered Hungarian dress and had him crowned as King of Hungary. As the archbishop placed the heavy gold crown of St Stephen on the boy's head Joseph sank under its weight and the crown slipped down to his ears. Ruling Hungary was going to be an equally heavy task for the Habsburgs.

Only slightly younger than Joseph was Francis Rakoczi, Prince of Transylvania. He had become a prisoner of war at the age of ten when his family castle had held out for two years against Leopold. Later he had travelled widely and on returning to Hungary as a young man he found his country helpless and miserable because of the plundering of Leopold's soldiers. He decided that the only hope was to get help from France but while trying to arrange this his plans were betrayed. He was imprisoned and sentenced to be beheaded. However, with the help of the captain of his guard he escaped, disguised as a dragoon and pretending to be very drunk. Eventually he reached Poland in safety.

Standard-bearer of the Kurucz army with Rakoczi's battle-flag. The Latin motto reads 'God does not desert a just cause'

Wars of the Spanish Succession

As the seventeenth century drew towards its close all Europe wondered what would happen to the vast territories owned by the Spanish branch of the Habsburg family when the present King of Spain died. In addition to Spain itself, their European possessions consisted of large parts of Italy and much of what is now Belgium and Luxemburg. But this was not all. Overseas the Spanish King ruled over a great part of South America, over what is now California, Florida, Mexico and Panama, and over the Philippine Islands. Charles II, an imbecile invalid who should have died at birth, would never have an heir. When at last he died in 1700 nobody thought of asking the Spaniards whom they wanted. It was to be a struggle between the Habsburgs and the Bourbons for this great prize.

Charles, Leopold's second son, wanted the throne for the Habsburgs. Louis XIV wanted it for his grandson, Philip. The British and their Dutch allies were chiefly concerned to see that no one European nation became too powerful. Since France was their chief enemy it was natural for them to ally with Leopold to prevent one man becoming king both of France and Spain. By 1702 Europe was again at war. This was the time when the English commander-in-chief, the Duke of Marlborough, made his famous march from the Netherlands, where his army was based, to the Danube. Here he joined forces with Prince Eugène to bar the way to the French who were advancing on Vienna. At Blenheim in 1704 the French were defeated and Vienna saved.

Meanwhile, the moment of danger for Leopold was the moment of opportunity for Hungary. Rakoczi was called home from Poland to lead a national revolt and everywhere Hungarians rose against their Austrian oppressors. After savage and bitter fighting Rakoczi was master of Hungary and even dared to send a raiding party to within a few miles of Vienna. In 1705 Leopold died and Joseph I was Emperor. For the next six years every county, castle and town was fought for with huge loss of life. Once again Rakoczi saw that Hungary must have help and he returned to Poland to raise an army. While he was there Joseph suddenly died of smallpox in 1711 and his brother Charles, still hoping for the Spanish throne, found himself the Emperor Charles VI.

From this moment the war petered out. The British no more wished to see the same man Emperor of Austria and King of Spain, as to see France and Spain ruled by one man. When it was agreed that if Philip became King of Spain he would never rule also in France, the war was over. At the Dutch town of Utrecht peace was signed in 1713. Charles VI had to abandon any hope of the Spanish throne but, as Emperor, he was also given the Netherlands and much territory in Italy to rule. As for Rakoczi, he never returned to Hungary but died in exile in Turkey. His legend as one of Hungary's national heroes lives on in the haunting music of the famous Rakoczi march.

*Marlborough with two of his foot-runners
at the Battle of Blenheim*

The duke gave his orders to one of his two runners who delivered it as fast as he could to the various commanders. They wore curious jockey caps, blue and yellow coats with sashes, and carried a long staff as a badge of office.

Imperial troops during the Seven Years War

"Our lives and blood"

Charles VI, an obstinate and unintelligent man, never got over the loss of the Spanish throne and brought to Vienna the fashions and manners of the Spanish court. Having lost Spain he was terrified that after his death the Habsburgs would lose Austria also. His heir was his beautiful daughter, Maria Theresa, barred as a woman from inheriting the Habsburg lands. Charles spent much of his reign persuading European sovereigns to promise to recognise her as ruler of the undivided Habsburg possessions on his death. He died in 1740 hoping that these promises would be kept.

Maria Theresa was now a young married woman, inexperienced in affairs of state, with an empty treasury and a weak army. Three months after her accession Frederick the Great of Prussia seized Silesia, one of the richest parts of the Austrian Empire. Within a year all promises had been broken. France wanted to rob Austria of the Netherlands and Luxemburg. Charles Albert of Bavaria wanted the Imperial Crown. The ruler of Saxony intended to get his share of the prey. The fortunes of Austria had never been so low.

Suddenly the tide turned. Maria Theresa at her coronation as Queen of Hungary in 1741 threw herself on the loyalty of her subjects. The reaction was immediate and decisive. The Hungarians shouted 'Our Lives and Blood' and drew their sabres to show their readiness to protect their young Queen. A few days later Maria Theresa presented the six months old Crown Prince Joseph to the assembled nobles. The child cried, and although Maria Theresa was later accused of pinching him, the sight of a beautiful mother with her crying baby strengthened the Hungarian determination to fight for Maria Theresa as they had never fought for a Habsburg before.

Spanish Riding School

The famous Lipizzaner horses of Vienna are a four-centuries-old breed. When born they are black and only on maturity do they gain their legendary grey-white colour. The Riding School, founded in 1735, still produces the finest horsemen and the best trained horses in the world. The perfect displays originally served a much more practical purpose. Some, like the pesade illustrated here, were mediaeval cavalry exercises used to terrify enemy infantry. During Maria Theresa's reign the riders wore red jackets with gold trimmings, which was a court uniform. The School was also used for coach driving exercises by fashionable ladies and gentlemen.

The Seven Years War

For much of the next twenty-five years Europe was at war. At first everything went wrong for Maria Theresa. The French, allied to Frederick the Great of Prussia, believed that the moment had come for the final triumph of Bourbons over Habsburgs. Prague was captured and Vienna was once again threatened. It was now that Maria Theresa made her great appeal to her subjects. With the loyal support of Austrians and Hungarians the invader was driven back. So successful was the Empress that with her British allies she planned an invasion of France across the Rhine. This remarkable turn of fortune was partly due to Maria Theresa's ability to arouse the loyal devotion of her people. It was even more due to the fact that for the moment Frederick the Great decided to withdraw from the war. All he wanted was Silesia and he had got it. If Maria Theresa would agree to surrendering the province she need not fear further Prussian attacks. To this she proudly refused to submit. The war dragged on with Frederick back in the fighting. By 1748 all nations were exhausted and a peace which settled nothing was signed.

There were really two separate wars going on at the same time. There was the age-old struggle for empire between France and Britain which was being fought out in India and Canada. There was the newer rivalry between the Habsburgs in Austria and the rising power of Prussia. Because of alliances the overseas war was also fought in Europe. The fact that the English King George II was also ruler of Hanover was another reason why British troops were on the continent.

When war broke out again in 1756, a war known to the British as the Seven Years War, the alliances were switched round. Immediate fear of Prussia forced Maria Theresa to make a strange alliance with her old enemy, France. Britain, mostly concerned with defeating France overseas, saw in Frederick a useful ally to keep the French occupied in Europe as well as abroad. Britain was able in 1759 to help Frederick by severely defeating the French at Minden near Hanover. Frederick was a brilliant soldier and a man of iron determination. He is rightly regarded as the founder of Prussia's greatness and thus the man whose work made it possible a century later for Prussia and not Austria to be the leading power in Europe. Throughout the fighting Frederick led his armies carrying in one pocket a bottle of poison in case he were captured, and in the other pocket his flute on which he loved to play. For Maria Theresa the war was a mixture of defeat and victory. She never succeeded in regaining Silesia but those who had tried to turn her off her throne had failed.

Fashions during Maria Theresa's reign

Despite the Wars of Succession the luxurious styles of French fashion gradually replaced the funereal Spanish court costumes of Leopold and Joseph I.

Maria Theresa set an example in her magnificent gold-embroidered costumes and even instituted a compulsory costume for her courtiers: red frock-coat worn over gold-embroidered waistcoat for men, red gown woven with gold and silver for ladies. In Poland and Hungary the nobility continued to wear the ancient national costumes, now even more elaborate.

Later in the eighteenth century Hungarian ladies adopted the fur-lined jacket ('pelisse') and fur hats of the Noble Guards' Hussar uniform.

Maria Theresa

Maria Theresa was very much a Queen. She was both a strong and imperious ruler of her subjects and at the same time a devoted wife and mother. In this she was very like Queen Victoria of England. Her husband, Francis of Lorraine, was a quietly pleasant man whom she made Emperor in 1745. As a woman she was unable to wear the imperial crown. Foreign diplomats at her court sometimes found it difficult to know how to treat Francis so as to please the Empress. She insisted that they should show him the same deference as they showed to her, but when it came to politics then it must be with her alone that they spoke. She had the gift of winning the passionate loyalty of her peoples. They admired her for her unfailing courage, her devotion to duty and her unshaken confidence in God. Her dignity was so natural that she never lost their respect because of her easy familiarity with those whom she met. Once in later years she actually walked in night attire from her rooms to the court theatre to tell the delighted Viennese that a grandson had been born on her birthday. When in 1765 Francis died Maria Theresa was heartbroken. She was only thirty-nine years old and had borne sixteen children. Over the years she had grown to rely on her kindly but unexciting husband and she never really recovered from his death. She cut short her lovely hair and as Queen Victoria would do a century later, she wore black for the rest of her life.

In her long reign of forty years Maria Theresa and her ministers brought prosperity to Austria and Hungary. Taxes were to be paid by everyone – though the Hungarians did not always obey. A new standing army was formed, well trained and equipped. It was she who built the splendid Schönbrunn Palace in Vienna, as well as other fine buildings in and around the city.

*Maria Theresa in the grounds of Schönbrunn Palace
with her son Joseph and Maria Christina.
In attendance is an officer of the Hungarian Noble Guard*

Joseph II tries his hand at ploughing

The Uncrowned King

Joseph II was the best example of an 'Enlightened Despot'. This meant an autocratic ruler determined to govern so as to help his poorer subjects. He became Emperor on his father's death in 1765 but only ruler of Austria when Maria Theresa died in 1780. He refused to be crowned lest his coronation oath should restrict his authority and was nicknamed 'The King with the Hat', as he liked to wear his tricorn hat on all occasions. Joseph was an attractive and intelligent man, simple in his tastes and devoted to improving the living conditions of the poor. One of his habits was to move in disguise among his subjects listening to their complaints and murmuring 'it won't be like this when I am king'. The trouble was that he was too far ahead of his time to succeed.

First the Catholic Church, then the nobility, were reformed. Bishops were chosen by Joseph, many monasteries were closed, services were to be in German and not Latin and all forms of Christian belief were tolerated. Special privileges enjoyed by the nobility were curtailed and the serfs who worked on their lands were freed. It was impossible for reforms carried through so quickly to succeed in a land where the Catholic Church and the nobility had always been all-powerful. Furthermore, in spite of his policy at home his adventures abroad had failed and by 1788 he was in a sea of troubles. Before he died in 1790 he had been forced to withdraw most of his reforms. Clergy and nobles were overjoyed but the legend grew that Joseph rose from his grave at night to continue his walks around his kingdom, watching over the welfare of his humblest subjects.

Mozart in Salzburg

Austria was a land of music. Gluck, composer of operas, lived at Maria Theresa's court. The princely family of Esterházy chose Haydn as their resident composer. Mozart was born in Salzburg where the Archbishop was his unkind patron. One of the greatest musicians of all time, in his short life of less than thirty-six years Mozart poured out symphonies, operas and compositions of every kind. Emperors and generals may be forgotten: Mozart's music will live for ever.

The Emperor Francis II

Francis II and the Napoleonic Wars

When Joseph II died unexpectedly his nephew, Francis, succeeded him after two years at the age of twenty-four. He ruled Austria for forty-five years and for twenty-five of those years he was at war with France. During the French Revolution of 1789–94 King Louis XVI and his Austrian wife, Marie Antoinette, daughter of Maria Theresa, had been executed. Now the French revolutionary armies were led by one of the greatest soldiers of all time, Napoleon. Francis II was an honourable, kindly, but not very clever man: yet this pale, thin-faced Emperor was resolutely dedicated to the overthrow of Napoleon. He knew how to bend before the storm and he survived all disasters.

Disasters came thick and fast. Napoleon's armies seemed invincible. Vienna was captured and in 1806 at Austerlitz the Austrian army was overwhelmed. Francis was forced to sign a treaty which brought three million Austrians under French rule. This was the moment when Napoleon declared that the Holy Roman Empire was at an end. It had long ceased to be more than a name. Unperturbed, Francis II decided that henceforth he would be called Emperor Francis I of Austria, Hungary and Bohemia.

Peace did not last long. Although Vienna was not again captured the Austrian army was defeated at Wagram. More Austrian lands were lost and Francis was even forced to marry his daughter to Napoleon, whom she detested. However, revenge was not far off. In 1812 Napoleon embarked on his disastrous invasion of Russia. His enemies united to bar his way home to France and in a three-day battle at Leipzig, fought in pouring rain, Napoleon was defeated, forced to abdicate and exiled to the island of Elba.

Vienna now became the brilliant setting for the famous Congress of 1814–15. Everybody of any importance came to Vienna: emperors, kings, princes, soldiers and statesmen. At night there were grand balls and receptions; by day the statesmen sat down to redraw the map of Europe. Suddenly news came that Napoleon had escaped and was advancing into Belgium. An allied army under the English Duke of Wellington finally destroyed Napoleon at Waterloo. The statesmen could return to their work and the mastermind behind the new Europe was Prince Metternich, Austria's evil genius.

Hussar of the Eighth Imperial Hussar Regiment, about 1809

*Swordfight between French Cuirassiers
and Austrian Dragoons*

The Battle of Wagram

Although the Austrian army was defeated at Wagram in 1809, it was not an overwhelming defeat like Austerlitz. In a deadly two-day battle hundreds were killed in bayonet charges and cavalry attacks. When it was all over the exhausted Napoleon found to his relief that the Austrians had withdrawn from the battlefield. Some time after the battle a French politician remarked to Napoleon that Austria was no longer a danger. To this Napoleon replied: 'It is evident that you were not on the field of Wagram.'

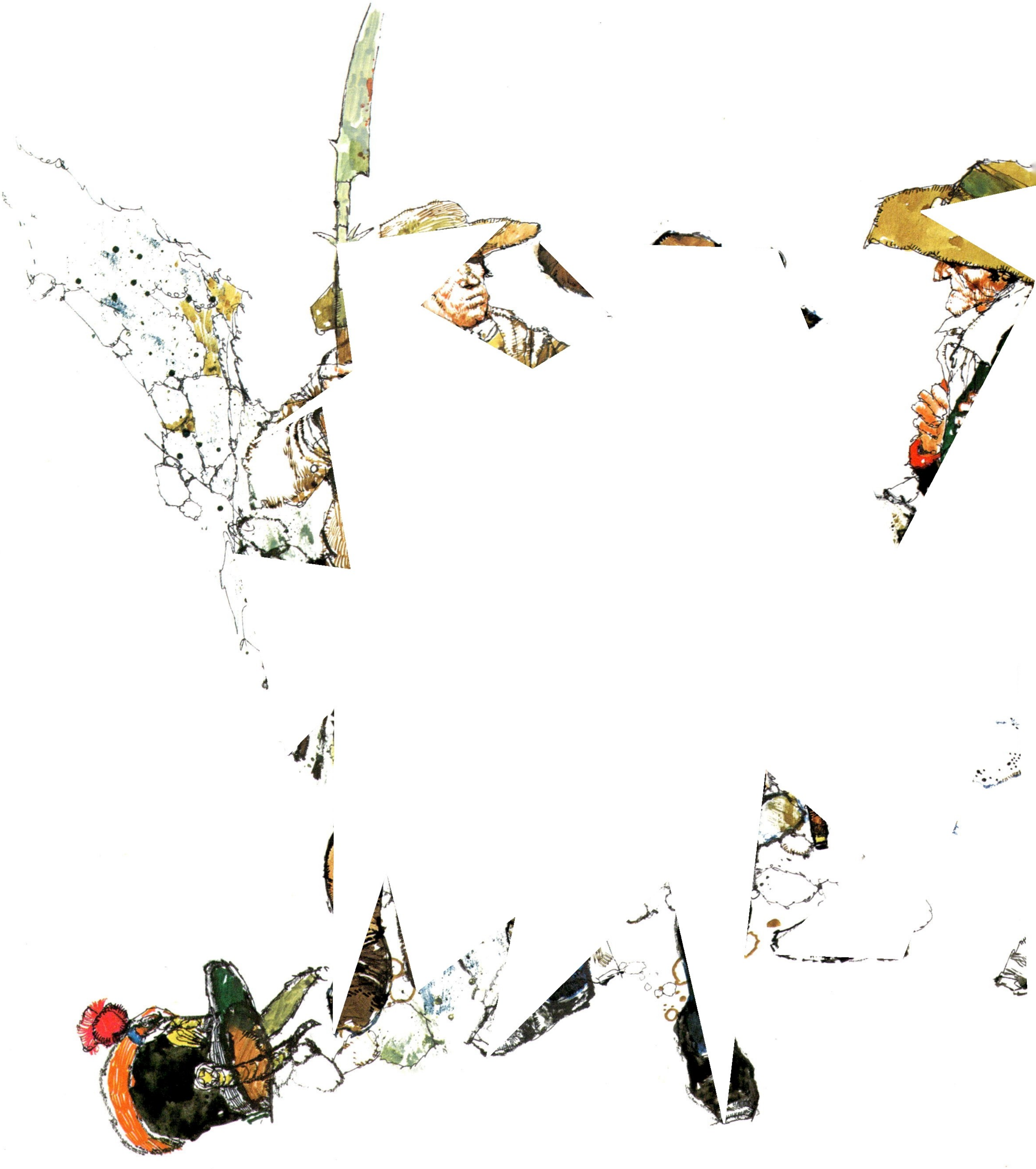

Andreas Hofer and the Tirol

Andreas Hofer, the great Tirolean patriot, was an innkeeper who joined the Austrian army to fight the French and rose to the rank of captain. After Austerlitz Napoleon gave Tirol to his allies, the Bavarians, and it was Hofer's burning desire to drive the Bavarians from his native soil. His opportunity came in 1808 when a popular rising broke out, led by an Austrian general who soon proved to be unsuccessful. Hofer took command and a huge peasant army gathered under his flag. His men had left their families and their mountain homes, armed with their hunting rifles or often with nothing more than crude weapons made from farm tools. This patriot army now joined battle with the Bavarians at Bergisel, near Innsbruck. For four days the fighting went on. Tirolean sharpshooters poured a deadly and accurate fire on the enemy while Hofer attacked from all sides. When the battle ended the Bavarians were in full retreat and within a year all Tirol was free.

Hofer had reckoned without his Emperor. Francis I signed an armistice with France and surrendered Tirol once again. Hofer and his men had no intention of accepting this surrender and succeeded in driving back a large force of French and Bavarians. In spite of this victory a further treaty confirmed the loss of Tirol and as French troops poured again into Tirol Hofer took to the mountains to wage guerrilla war. He knew that he could expect no help from Francis. When Hofer was eventually betrayed and captured Francis did not lift a finger to save him. Napoleon had him court-martialled and executed at Mantua in 1810. Later his body was brought back to Innsbruck for honourable burial in the Court Chapel.

Beethoven with St Stephen's Cathedral in the background

Beethoven in Vienna

Beethoven was a composer of genius who ranks in music on the same level as Shakespeare in poetry. He was a German born in Bonn in 1770, who came to live in Vienna in 1792. Unlike earlier composers he did not attach himself to a rich patron but made his own concert engagements and music publishing contracts. At the same time he had to rely for support on a number of wealthy friends in Vienna who quickly recognised his brilliance as a pianist and later his greatness as a composer. Much of his life was tragic. He never married, though he wanted to do so; he was badly treated by his nephew whom he had befriended; as he grew older he suffered from continuous ill health and increasing deafness. However, nothing stopped him from creating great music. He had been at first a great admirer of Napoleon and dedicated his third symphony, known as the 'Eroica', to him. His admiration turned to disgust when Napoleon made himself Emperor. His genius was recognised in his lifetime and during the Congress of Vienna royalty and statesmen paid tribute by attending a performance of his only opera 'Fidelio'. He died in 1827.

Fashions in Vienna during the Napoleonic Wars

Like Paris and London, Vienna was a major fashion centre at the beginning of the nineteenth century. The Napoleonic wars did not prevent elegant young ladies of Vienna appearing in some of the finest Empire-line costumes in Europe.

The Congress of Vienna gave even more of an excuse for glitter and extravaganza in costumes, as the crowned heads of Europe gathered in the city.

The ladies in this illustration are wearing sun-bonnets and gowns designed for the fashion journal 'Vienner Moden' (Viennese Fashion) and the officer wears the red and white regulation uniform of a Field Marshal, complete with tall cocked hat with green plumes indicating his rank.

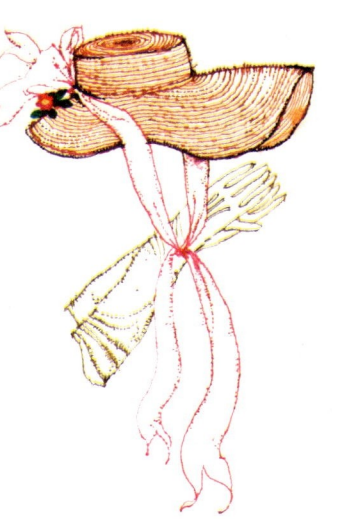

The Emperor Ferdinand and Prince Metternich

Metternich and the Year of Revolution: 1848

Metternich hated change and dreaded revolution. He hoped to put the clock back to the days before the French Revolution. To do this he formed an alliance, known as the 'Holy Alliance', between Austria, Prussia and Russia. Each nation promised to come to the help of any one of them who was attacked by an enemy power. Thus a nation trying to dominate Europe, as Napoleon had done, would at once be met by three united armies. Of more immediate importance was the agreement to help each other suppress any kind of revolutionary activity within their countries. Francis approved of this and supported Metternich's policy of turning Austria and Hungary into countries where police spies listened for any one talking against the government and where newspapers and public meetings were rigidly censored. Metternich became even more powerful after Francis died in 1835 as the new emperor, Ferdinand, was weak in mind. Nevertheless, opposition to Metternich and his methods of government grew. The new working class in their factories demanded better conditions. Writers and other intellectuals eagerly listened to revolutionary ideas once again coming from France. Even aristocrats and army officers began to question the autocratic way their country was governed.

In 1848 the storm broke. Another revolution in Paris sparked off revolutions in other European capitals. The Hungarians found a leader in the fiery orator Kossuth, who for nearly ten years had been demanding an end to the crushing Habsburg rule. Debates in parliament still took place in Latin; the aristocracy were still free from paying taxes as in the Middle Ages; no man was free to speak his mind. Budapest revolted and Vienna quickly followed. The hated Metternich escaped with a forged passport, never to return.

Gunner of the Artillery, Hungarian National Army

Eventually, amid chaos and confusion, a ruthless woman took charge. She was Sophie of Bavaria, wife of the heir to the throne, the Archduke Charles. She persuaded the pathetic Emperor Ferdinand to abdicate in favour not of her husband but of her son, Franz Joseph. She restored the old repressive policy and inspired her son to take ruthless revenge on the rebels.

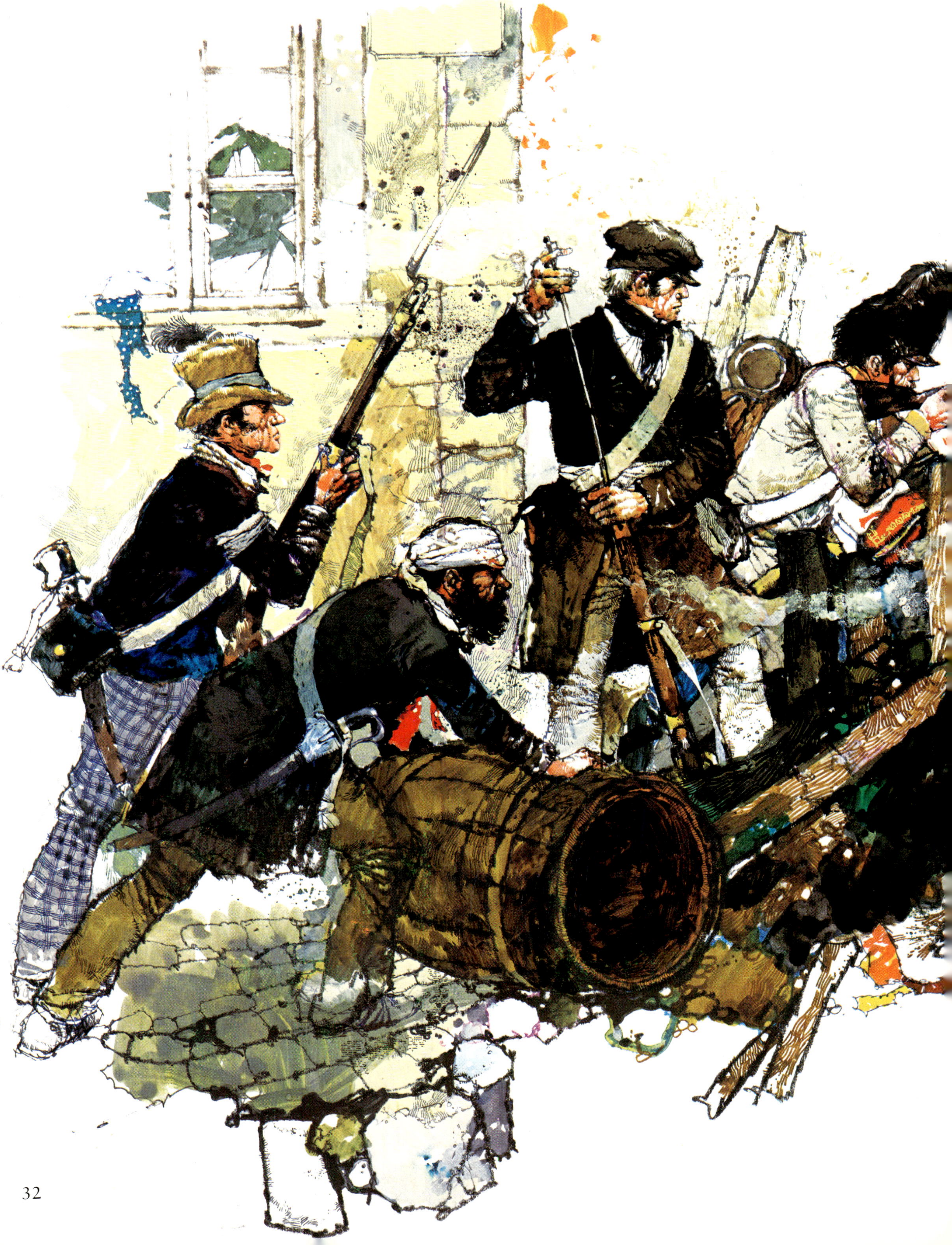

Recovering from their first panic, the Habsburgs called to their aid the Croat general, Jellačic. In December 1848 students, citizens and soldiers forming the National Guard made a last stand in the narrow streets. A desperate call for help from the Hungarians came too late. Vienna was ceaselessly bombarded and cannons blasted the makeshift barricades. In a few days all was over. Government troops rounded up the few unshaven, bandaged and exhausted National Guard who remained alive. Some had managed to escape to form the Vienna Legion and to carry on the fight in Hungary. The Polish General Bem, one of Kossuth's best soldiers, escaped disguised as a cab driver, driving his carriage right through the enemy lines.

The last barricades in Vienna, 1848

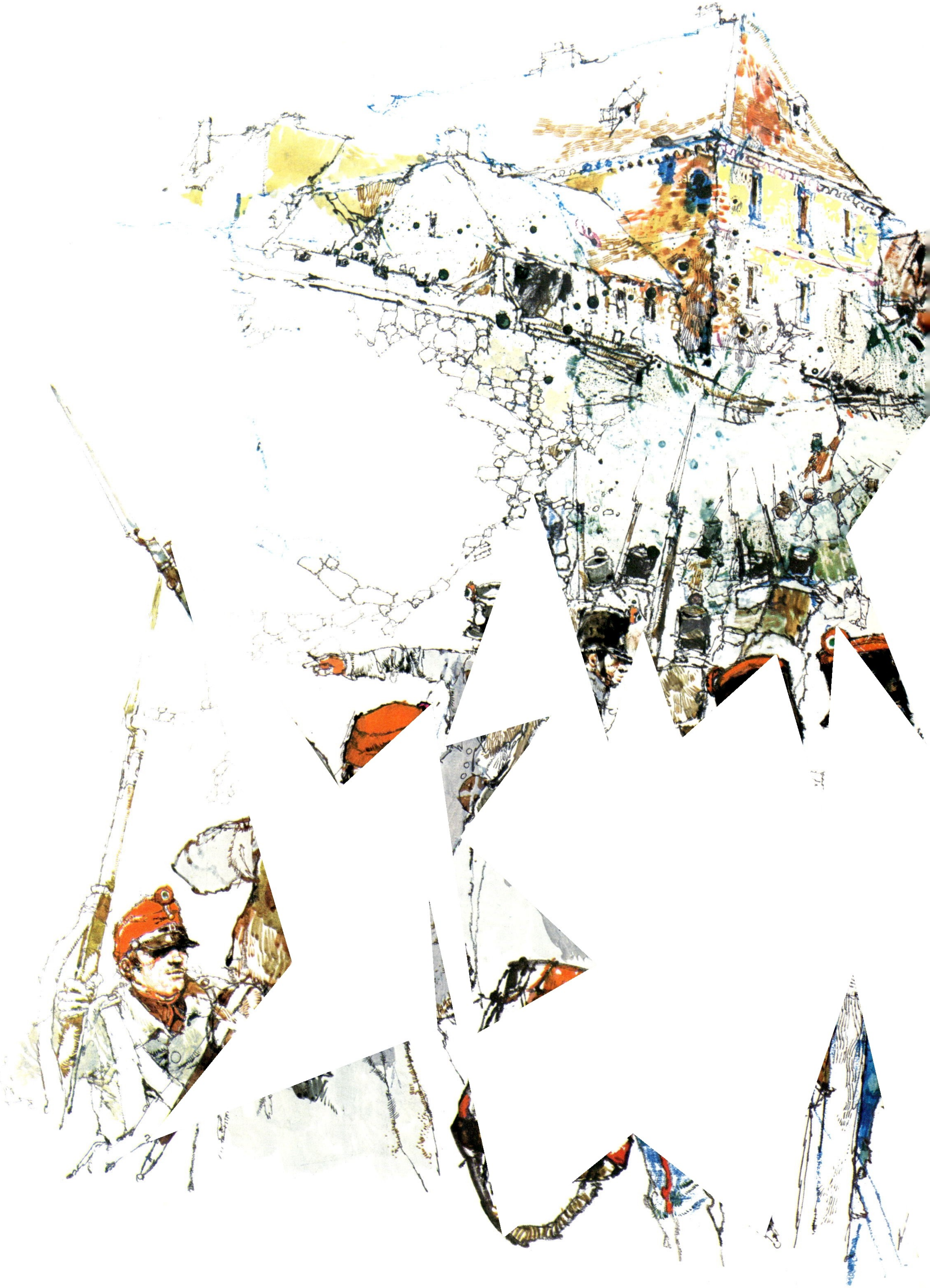

The capture of Buda castle was a matter of national pride to the Hungarians. After long and heavy bombardment the walls were breached. A rocket gave the signal for the night attack. As dawn broke the Hungarians fought their way through the breach and out of the mist the Hungarian flag was seen flowing out at the top of the citadel. The citizens of Buda were jubilant but already a Russian army was on its way to help Austria.

Buda Castle, 21 May 1849

Franz Joseph and the Dowager Empress

Franz Joseph: The Early Years

The Revolutions were broken. Franz Joseph began as an Emperor after his mother's heart, arrogant and autocratic. Disasters to his country and his family throughout his long reign turned him into a humbler man, whom his subjects came to respect. His beautiful wife Elizabeth, Queen of Hungary, never returned his love and preferred travelling to life in Vienna. She was struck down by an Italian assassin at Lake Geneva in 1898. His son, Rudolf, was to cause him intense grief. Within his Empire there was great unrest as the many races struggled to be independent. Abroad Austria was being challenged in Italy and by Prussia, now ruled by her Iron Chancellor, Bismarck.

Under the leadership of the tiny Kingdom of Piedmont and helped by France, Italians were determined to drive the Austrians out of northern Italy so as to be a free and united nation. In June 1859 after an Austrian defeat at Magenta Franz Joseph personally took command only to be even more seriously defeated at Solferino. This battle had two results. Austria lost control of Lombardy and a young Swiss banker, Henri Durant, who saw the horrors of the battlefield, founded the Red Cross Society to relieve suffering. More serious was the growing might of Prussia. Bismarck intended that henceforward Prussia and not Austria would dominate the new Germany and in 1866 in the Six Weeks War the Austrian army was overwhelmed at Königgrätz.

If Austria were to survive Franz Joseph must do something to satisfy the demands for independence within the Empire. In 1867 the Dual Monarchy of Austria-Hungary came into existence. It was a partnership of two nations after centuries of stormy contact. Franz Joseph, Emperor of Austria, now became also King of Hungary. The partnership was to last until 1918.

*Elizabeth at Bad Ischl,
the Imperial Hunting Lodge*

The Battery of the Dead, 3 July 1866

One of the most tragic incidents in the battle of Königgrätz was the destruction of the 7th Battery of the 8th Regiment of Horse Artillery. The Austrian cannons came under deadly accurate fire from Prussian infantry and most of the batteries were ordered to withdraw to avoid further losses. One battery under the command of Captain von Groeten stayed to fight a rearguard action. Most of the men came from south-east Hungary. The captain left just enough soldiers to fire the guns and led the rest in a suicidal bayonet charge against the massing Prussians. They were all killed. The guns kept firing until all the crew was shot down. One man and one officer survived out of the whole battery and reached the Austrian lines. As dawn broke over the deserted battlefield the soldiers of the Battery of the Dead were found lying next to their guns. Not one ran away, not one surrendered.

Johann Strauss I with his father's inn 'The Good Shepherd' in the background

Kings of the Waltz

Johann Strauss, son of a Viennese innkeeper was born in 1804. As a child he listened for hours to travelling violin players in his father's inn. His parents died while he was quite young but a kind stepfather had given him an old fiddle on which to practise. This he treasured greatly and soaked it in beer to improve its tone. Later he took proper lessons and joined the orchestra of a well known violinist, Joseph Lanner. Strauss soon surpassed Lanner both as player and composer of waltzes. His fame spread through Europe which became waltz mad. The dance was not new but had been regarded as scandalous because a man had to seize his partner tightly round the waist. The Viennese waltz was welcomed as delightful and refined and everyone danced it to Strauss's melodies. However, two events broke his glittering career. His son Johann Strauss II, proved to be an even greater musician and openly challenged his father as Waltz King. The other tragedy was the revolution of 1848 which divided father and son still further. Johann I composed the Radetsky March in honour of the general who had so brutally stamped out the revolution. Johann II had fought with the rebels. Broken-hearted, Johann I died in 1849.

Johann Strauss II was now undisputed Waltz King. In 1867 he composed the famous 'Blue Danube' waltz. Fame and fortune came not only throughout Europe but also in America. Here he conducted a colossal orchestra and choir of nearly 20,000 in return for an equally large fee. More triumphs followed and he was honoured by the Emperor and by the city of Vienna which he and his father had made the home of the waltz. He died in 1899.

Franz Joseph: The Later Years

Franz Joseph, seen here in his Hungarian general's uniform, remained an impressive figure, even in old age. He ate very little and very fast. His guests often left hungry because they could not keep up with his speed of eating. He always slept on a hard, iron bed and began his day's work at 5 a.m. He worked on through lunch, eating as he read. He lived a very isolated life; his sole relaxation was hunting, which he preferred to do alone. A lonely old man whose life was full of tragedies, his long reign lasted into a world which he did not understand.

Franz Joseph in Hungarian Field Marshal's uniform, about 1880

The Archduke Rudolf and Maria Vetsera with Mayerling Lodge in the background

Mayerling

In the morning of 29 January 1889 the Archduke Rudolf of Austria was found dead together with his eighteen-year-old mistress Maria Vetsera. The scandal rocked the Empire and Europe. Rudolf, who inherited his mother's good looks and charm, was an intelligent, likeable young man, popular with everyone except his father. Soon he acquired a reputation as a liberal and became closely involved with Hungarian radicals. Franz Joseph deliberately isolated Rudolf and accused him of disloyalty. Disillusioned, by the time he was thirty Rudolf suffered from severe depression. On 28 January he set out for his hunting lodge, Mayerling, where he made a suicide pact with Maria, and the next night they were dead. A revolver and farewell letters were found by the bedside.

The Millennium of 1896

The 'Millennium', or one thousandth anniversary of the founding of the Kingdom of Hungary, gave an excuse for much celebration, pomp and pageantry. Exhibitions and displays were held all over Budapest and memorials were erected to commemorate the event. Everybody who was anybody wore splendid national costumes based on the fashions of the seventeenth and eighteenth centuries, reflecting the growing wealth and national pride in the country.

Wine, Women and Song

In the 1890's Vienna was the fourth largest capital in Europe and a delightful city in which to live. You could drink coffee and read the papers in the comfortable Viennese coffee houses, or eat Madame Sacher's rich cakes while admiring the latest fashions paraded by elegant society ladies driving along the Ringstrasse. This famous circular road had been built after Franz Joseph had agreed in 1857 to the pulling down of the old city walls. Almost overnight palaces, museums and other buildings in every possible style of architecture lined the road. Everywhere there was music. Operas, concerts, Court balls and balls for charities were all the rage. In addition, operetta was always a popular form of entertainment in Vienna, and one of its most notable composers was Franz Lehar, born in 1870. His music combined the elegance of the waltz with the vigorous folk-music of his native Hungary. It was not surprising that the airs from his 'Merry Widow', first performed in 1905, swept Europe. Just outside the city was the Prater, a great park with a fun-fair, boating lake, illuminations by night and the great wheel from London's Crystal Palace revolving slowly to the latest tunes. Here all classes gathered. Members of fashionable society raced teams of horses on the Prater carriage way, while chamber-maids and off-duty soldiers strolled arm-in-arm. Vienna was not just a city of pleasure. New methods of painting were being explored by Klimt and his friends. More important work was taking place in the surgery of Dr Freud as he laid the foundations of modern psychology. Yet on the surface Vienna appeared carefree as the Viennese danced the nights away to the lilt of Strauss's 'Wine, Women and Song' waltz almost as if they knew that this gaiety could not last for ever.

Franz Lehar

The tunic worn by the Archduke Ferdinand

Gavrilo Princip, the assassin who fired the shots

Sarajevo: 28 June 1914

Franz Joseph's heir was the Archduke Franz Ferdinand, ruthless and autocratic, the most feared man in the Empire. As a hunter he was a deadly shot and delighted in slaughtering hundreds of thousands of animals and birds. One of his few redeeming features was his devotion to his Czech wife, who was regarded as an upstart by the Habsburgs for not being of royal blood. She was not allowed to sit in the royal box at the opera or to sit at the head of her dinner table if they were present. Six years earlier Austria had annexed the state of Bosnia which had wanted to unite with Serbia. Franz Ferdinand decided to inspect the Bosnian army and foolishly chose the Serbian national day for the inspection. Several students decided to try to shoot him. In the morning of the visit a bomb was thrown which only injured some officers and bystanders. In the afternoon Franz Ferdinand insisted on visiting the wounded in hospital. His driver took the wrong turning and the car stopped. By tragic coincidence this was the very moment that one of the students, Gavrilo Princip, found himself alongside the car. Before he could be stopped he had fired his pistol point blank at the Archduke and his wife and killed them. Austria decided to avenge their murder and declared war on Serbia. Russia, Serbia's ally, came to her aid. Within a month the First World War had begun.

Uniforms of the Imperial-Royal Army

On the left: Parade tunic of a Lieutenant of the 64th Imperial-Royal Infantry Regiment with tall black 'shako' decorated with gilt double eagle and gold braid. On the right: Hungarian general's parade 'attila' with 'pelisse' jacket and tall fur 'busby' with white plumes. This uniform is based on eighteenth-century Hussar dress in the Hungarian army.

The Emperor Charles in 1916

Fall of the Double Eagle

What had been planned as a little war to teach Serbia a lesson became a European struggle between the Central Powers, Germany and Austria-Hungary, and the Allies, Britain, France, Russia and Italy. Austria-Hungary found herself fighting Russia along a huge Eastern front stretching from Serbia through the Carpathian mountains to Poland. Although the Russians were held and thrown back, the losses in men and equipment were enormous. Gone were the days of glorious cavalry charges: instead, the Imperial Army had to face trench warfare in freezing southern Russia, where frost-bite and disease caused more loss of life than the actual fighting. Italy had entered the war in 1915 and a joint Austro-German army had to wage a particularly vicious and difficult campaign in the Alps. Franz Joseph had never intended warfare on this scale. Lonely and broken-hearted, he died in November 1916 after reigning for sixty-eight years. When he died, Imperial Austria died with him.

The new Emperor, Charles, carried on with the fight but the whole Empire grew increasingly war-weary. Troops were deserting and returning home. It was even difficult to find enough men to guard the Emperor or Vienna properly. In November 1918 both the German and the Austrian home-fronts collapsed. The Imperial Army was never finally defeated in battle but the will to carry on the war had gone. Unrest grew in Vienna and the Socialists demanded that the Emperor should abdicate. The Empire split in two as Austria and Hungary declared themselves to be republics. On 9 November Charles signed the document of abdication. Two days later two large cars drew up outside Schönbrunn Palace. Charles left Austria, never to return. The Habsburgs and their Double Eagle had passed into history.

*St Stephen's Crown, the Royal Crown of Hungary.
Presented by Pope Sylvester II.
Used to crown every Hungarian King from the 10th century
until 1916. The cross on top was damaged during the 17th century
and left that way ever since.*

Index

Battles:
   Austerlitz, 1806, *22*
   Blenheim, 1704, *12, 13*
   Königgrätz, 1866, *36, 38, 39*
   Magenta, 1859, *36*
   Minden, *16*
   Solferino, 1859, *36*
   Wagram, 1809, *25*
   Zenta, 1699, *7*
Beethoven, Ludwig van, *28*
Bem, General, *33*
Bismarck, Prince Otto von, *36*
Buda, *7, 9, 35*

Charles, Duke of Lorraine, *3*
Charles I, Emperor of Austria and King of Hungary, 1916–1918
   abdication, *46*
Charles II, King of Spain, *12*
Charles VI, Emperor of Austria and King of Hungary, 1711–1740, *12, 14*

Dual Monarchy of Austria-Hungary, *36*

Elizabeth, Empress of Austria and Queen of Hungary, *36, 37*
Eugène, Prince of Savoy, *6, 7, 9, 12*

Fashion, *17, 29*
Ferdinand, Emperor of Austria, King of Hungary 1835–1848, *30*
Francis I, Emperor of Austria, 1745–1765, *18*
Francis II, (Emperor Francis I of Austria, Hungary and Bohemia) 1790–1835, *22, 27, 30*
Franz Ferdinand, Archduke, assassination, *44*
Franz Joseph, Emperor of Austria, and King of Hungary after 1867, 1848–1916, *31, 36, 41, 42, 44*

Frederick the Great, King of Prussia, *16*
Freud, Dr Sigmund, *43*

George II, King of England, *16*
Gluck, *21*
Groeten, Captain von, *39*

Haydn, Joseph, *21*
Hofer, Andreas, *27*
Hungarians, *3, 7, 9, 12, 14, 30, 33, 35*
Hussars, *4, 5, 23*

Janissaries, *3*
Jellačic, *33*
John Sobieski, King of Poland, *3, 6*
Joseph, I, King of Hungary, Emperor of Austria, 1705–1711, *10, 12*
Joseph II, Emperor of Austria, King of Hungary 1780–1790, *14, 20, 22*

Kara Mustafa, Grand Vizier of Turkey, *3*
Kossuth, Louis, *30, 33*

Lehar, Franz, *43*
Leopold I, Emperor of Austria, 1658–1705, *2, 3, 6, 10, 12*
Lipizzaner Horses, *15*

Maria Theresa, Empress of Austria & Queen of Hungary 1740–1780, *14, 16, 17, 18, 19, 20*
Marlborough, Duke of, *12, 13*
Mayerling, *42*
Metternich, Prince, *23, 30*
Mozart, Wolfgang, *21*
Music, *21, 28, 40, 43*

Napoleon I, Emperor of France, *22, 23, 25, 27, 28*

Princip, Gavrilo, *44*

Rakoczi, Francis Prince of Transylvania, *10, 12*
Red Cross Society, *36*
Revolution:
   French, *22*
   Years of 1848, *30, 33*
Rudolf, Archduke of Austria, *36, 42*

Sarajevo, *44*
Strauss I, Johann, *40*
Strauss II, Johann, *40, 43*

Tirol, *27*
Turks, *3, 5, 9, 10*

Uniforms, *15, 29, 41, 45*
Utrecht, peace of, *12*

Vienna, *6, 15, 18, 43*
   siege of, *3, 5*
   captured, *22*
   congress of, *23, 29*
   revolution in, *30*
   Waltz, *40*

Wars:
   against Turks, *3, 5, 9*
   of Spanish Succession (1702–1713), *12*
   Seven Years (1756–1763), *16*
   Napoleonic (1798–1815), *22, 23, 25, 27, 29*
   Six Weeks (1866), *36*
   First World (1914–1918), *44, 46*

Under the Double Eagle

The title of this book is taken from the famous military march of the Austro-Hungarian Empire, Under the Double Eagle. It is well known in England as the Regimental March of the Queen's Dragoon Guards, a regiment that once had Franz Joseph as its Colonel-in-Chief and which to this day carries the Habsburg Double Eagle as its emblem.

This book is dedicated with love and gratitude to my Mother, and to the memory of my Father

Oxford University Press, Walton Street, Oxford OX2 6DP

OXFORD LONDON GLASGOW
NEW YORK TORONTO MELBOURNE WELLINGTON
KUALA LUMPUR SINGAPORE HONG KONG TOKYO
DELHI BOMBAY CALCUTTA MADRAS KARACHI
NAIROBI DAR ES SALAAM CAPE TOWN

© Victor G. Ambrus 1979   ISBN 0 19 279722 0

Library of Congress Catalogue Card Number: 78–41179

All rights reserved. No part of this publication may be reproduced, stored in a retrieval system, or transmitted, in any form or by any means, electronic, mechanical, photocopying, recording, or otherwise, without the prior permission of Oxford University Press

Photoset in Sabon by Western Printing Services Ltd, Bristol
Printed in Hong Kong by Bright Sun Printing Press